Birds

ANN O. SQUIRE

Children's Press®
An Imprint of Scholastic Inc.
New York Toronto London Auckland Sydney
Mexico City New Delhi Hong Kong
Danbury, Connecticut

Content Consultant
Stephen S. Ditchkoff, PhD
Professor of Wildlife Sciences
Auburn University
Auburn, Alabama

Library of Congress Cataloging-in-Publication Data
Squire, Ann.
 Birds / Ann O. Squire.
  p. cm.—(A true book)
 Summary: "This book covers the habits, physical features, reproduction, and life cycle of
birds."— Provided by publisher.
 Audience: 9–12.
 Audience: Grades 4 to 6.
 ISBN 978-0-531-21751-1 (lib. bdg.) — ISBN 978-0-531-22336-9 (pbk.)
 1. Birds—Juvenile literature. I. Title. II. Series: True book.
 QL676.2.S65 2014
 598—dc23   2013002136

Front cover: Common buzzards
Back cover: A red-legged seriema

Find the Truth!

Everything you are about to read is true *except* for one of the sentences on this page.

Which one is **TRUE**?

T or F All birds migrate.

T or F All birds lay eggs.

Find the answers in this book.

3

Contents

1 What Do These Animals Have in Common?

Are penguins, hummingbirds,
and ostriches related? 7

2 Meet the Birds

What characteristics make a bird a bird? 15

3 Different Habitats, Different Birds

How are waterbirds different
from perching birds? 25

THE BIG TRUTH!

Birds and Oil Spills

Why are oil spills so destructive to bird
populations? 30

4

A group of macaws perches in the forest.

4 Courtship and Mating
What kinds of nests do birds build? 33

5 Humans and Birds
Why should humans care about birds? 39

True Statistics 44
Resources 45
Important Words 46
Index 47
About the Author 48

Only male peacocks have brightly colored feathers.

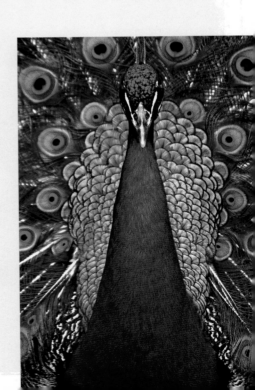

Gentoo penguins live along the Antarctic coast and nearby islands.

What Do These Animals Have in Common?

On a deserted, snow-covered beach on the continent of Antarctica, a black-and-white penguin waddles toward the water. Behind it are many other penguins, all heading in the same direction. Their movements are clumsy and slow. It seems that they are not quite at home on land. Reaching a rocky ledge, the lead penguin pauses for a moment. Then it tips forward and dives headfirst into the icy ocean waters.

A Swimming Machine

The penguin's smooth, torpedo-shaped body slips through the waves with ease. Using its wings as flippers and its feet and tail to steer, the penguin "flies" underwater at up to 15 miles (24.1 kilometers) per hour. As it swims, the penguin looks out for fish and **krill**. Making a quick turn, it grabs a fish in its hooked beak. The penguin swallows the fish in one gulp and darts away to find another meal.

A gentoo penguin dives up to 450 times a day for food.

8

Thanks to its fast-moving wings, this green violet-ear hummingbird can hover in the air.

Feeding on Nectar

In a lush Central American garden, a hummingbird searches for something to eat. At each new flower, the little bird hovers in midair. Its tiny wings beat more than 50 times per second. Few flowers have what the hummingbird is looking for. More often than not, the bird backs away and heads in a new direction. Hummingbirds are amazingly agile. Most birds can fly only forward. A hummingbird can fly backward, up, down, and even sideways!

A hummingbird can eat twice its body weight in a day.

A Feathery Tongue

The hummingbird finds a large plant with bright red, tube-shaped flowers. Hovering, the bird thrusts its long beak into a flower. The hummingbird's tongue is even longer than its beak and can reach the bottom of the nectar-filled blossom. The tongue is forked at the end and covered with feathery fringe, perfect for scooping up nectar. A hummingbird dips its tongue into a flower up to 15 times per second before flitting to the next flower.

Big Birds

On the plains of East Africa, a mother ostrich leads its chicks through the underbrush. Nearby, its mate keeps watch for predators. Suddenly, something catches the male's attention. A tawny lioness creeps through the grass toward the mother and chicks. Rather than hiding, the father ostrich flaps its wings and walks unsteadily in the opposite direction. By pretending to be sick or injured, it may be able to distract the lioness and save its young.

Two ostriches watch over their young chicks.

11

The lioness takes a look at the limping ostrich and goes back to stalking the mother and chicks. If it cannot lead the lioness away, the male's only choice is to confront the predator. Approaching the lioness, it strikes out with its powerful legs. The larger of the two toes on each foot ends in a long claw. A well-placed kick could kill the lioness. Faced with the huge, angry ostrich, the lioness slinks away.

Ostriches have a powerful kick that they use against any possible threats, from lions to humans to giraffes.

What do these giant ostriches have in common with tiny hummingbirds and sleek penguins?

Same or Different?

These three animals seem completely different from one another. The penguin moves around by swimming, the hummingbird by flying, and the ostrich by running. The hummingbird weighs just a few ounces, while the ostrich can weigh more than 300 pounds (136.1 kilograms). The penguin's body is rounded and heavy, and the hummingbird's is delicate and light. What can all three creatures possibly have in common?

CHAPTER 2

Meet the Birds

Penguins, hummingbirds, and ostriches may seem very different from the pigeons in your local park or the robins in your backyard. However, they have a lot in common: they are all birds. Birds are members of the **class** Aves. Within this class, there are about 10,000 different species. Birds are found on every continent on Earth. They can survive in habitats ranging from tropical rain forests to dry deserts to polar ice caps.

A male peacock's long tail feathers are called a train.

What Makes a Bird a Bird?

In many ways, birds are similar to humans. Like humans, birds are **vertebrates**. Humans and birds breathe air and are **endothermic**. They also have four limbs—people have legs and arms, while birds have legs and wings. That is where the similarities end. Humans are specialized for life on land. Birds are specialized for life in the air. All birds have characteristics that are related to flight, though not all birds use them to fly.

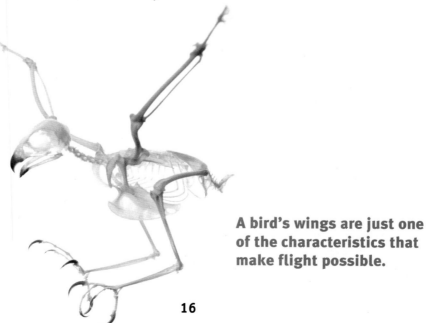

A bird's wings are just one of the characteristics that make flight possible.

A puffin makes a careful, controlled landing among a gathering of other puffins.

A Lightweight Skeleton

In order to fly, a bird's body needs to be as light as possible. Birds have bones, but they are much less heavy and dense than those of land animals. The bones of flying birds are thin-walled and hollow. Sometimes the bones have cross walls, or struts, for added strength. Many of a bird's bones are fused together. This makes the skeleton rigid and strong enough to withstand takeoffs and landings.

Swallows need speed and agility to catch the insects they hunt for food.

On the Wing

All birds have wings. Wings come in different shapes and sizes. Hawks, crows, and many backyard birds have short, rounded wings. These let them move easily around trees and other vegetation. Long-distance flyers, such as albatrosses, have long, narrow wings to glide over the ocean. High-speed flyers, such as swallows and falcons, have long, pointed wings. Penguins, which do not fly, use their wings as small but powerful flippers.

Feathered Friends

The bodies of all birds are covered with feathers. Birds that fly have long, stiff flight feathers on their wings and tails. These feathers create an **airfoil** that helps lift a bird off the ground. Contour feathers cover the bird's body, overlapping like shingles on a roof. These feathers shed rain, keeping the animal dry. Fluffy down feathers lie beneath the contour feathers. Like a down jacket, down feathers keep the bird warm.

Regular preening, or cleaning, keeps a bird's feathers in good shape.

19

Colored Feathers

Feathers come in a range of colors. In some species, such as American goldfinches, males use color to attract females during mating season. In spring, the male goldfinch sports bright yellow and black **plumage**. At other times of year, its feathers are mostly gray. Some birds use their plumage to blend in. In winter, a willow ptarmigan is white and almost invisible against the snow. In spring and summer, its feathers are dull, mottled brown.

Male goldfinches use their bright spring colors to catch the attention of a female.

Cardinals often use vines, even poison ivy vines, to build nests.

Laying Eggs

All birds reproduce by laying eggs. Eggs are **incubated** until they hatch. Birds cannot give birth to live young the way people do. In animals that bear live young, the mother gains weight as the baby develops inside her. For a mother bird, this would be a disaster—she would be too heavy to fly. Soon after an egg forms inside her body, she lays it. A hard shell protects the developing chick inside.

A warbler's pointed beak is good for picking up insects from twigs and leaves.

Toothless

As another adaptation to life in the air, birds do not have teeth. Teeth add weight. Instead, birds have a lightweight beak, also called a bill. Birds' beaks are specialized for the food they eat. Insect eaters such as warblers have slender, pointed beaks. Owls, hawks, and other birds of prey have sharp, hooked beaks. Finches have cone-shaped beaks that are strong enough to crack seeds. Hummingbirds have long, thin beaks that reach deep inside a flower.

Quick Facts about Some Common Birds

Group	Characteristics	Diet	Distribution	Life Span
Waterfowl, such as ducks, geese, and swans (about 180)	Large aquatic birds with webbed feet; most are strong flyers; some have been domesticated	Grass, leaves, aquatic plants, insects, small fish	Worldwide, except Antarctica	Most live around 10–20 years
Penguins (about 20)	Flightless; wings modified into flippers; strong swimmers; black-and-white coloration	Fish, krill	Southern Hemisphere, Antarctic and sub-Antarctic regions, coastal South America, and southern Africa	10–20 years
Raptors, such as falcons, hawks, and eagles (about 300)	Talons, hooked bills, keen eyesight, broad wings	Small mammals, birds, fish, reptiles, insects, frogs, lizards	Worldwide, except Antarctica	10–30 years, depending on the species
Parrots, parakeets, and cockatoos (about 400)	Strong, curved bill; strong feet adapted for climbing and grasping food; all nest in tree hollows	Mostly fruit and seeds, some insects	Tropical regions of South and Central America, Africa, Asia, Australia, New Zealand	Smaller species often live around 20–40 years; larger parrots can live 70 years or longer
Owls (about 230)	Strong talons, sharp downward-curving beak, acute hearing and eyesight; nocturnal hunters; feathers adapted for silent flight	Rodents and other small mammals, birds, insects	Worldwide, except Antarctica	Around 20 years
Passerines, or perching birds, such as sparrows, jays, and robins (about 4,300)	Small body size; feet specialized for perching; most species sing complex songs	Seeds, insects, nectar, sometimes fruit	Worldwide, except Antarctica	Usually around 5–10 years

Birds of paradise are found in the forests of New Guinea, Australia, and surrounding islands.

CHAPTER 3

Different Habitats, Different Birds

Birds are found on every continent. Birds are warm-blooded. Their body temperature is constant, even when the outside temperature is very hot or cold. This helps birds survive in many different environments. Penguins, some of which live in Earth's coldest climate, have a layer of fat beneath the skin to keep them warm. They also have tightly packed feathers, which they coat with oil from a gland near the tail. This makes the feathers almost waterproof.

 Passerines generally hop instead of walking.

Birds in the Trees

Many birds are found in trees. Perching birds, or passerines, have special adaptations to life in the treetops. They have four toes, three facing forward and one facing backward. This allows them to cling to branches and tree trunks. When a passerine bird goes to sleep, its toes automatically tighten on its perch. This way, the bird can sleep without falling. Passerines are also small. They can maneuver easily and land on thin branches.

Perching birds make up more than half the world's bird species.

Much like penguins, ducks and other waterfowl coat their feathers with a special oil to make them waterproof.

Adapted to the Water

Ducks, geese, and other waterfowl have webbed feet to paddle through the water. Ducks have flattened bills with bumps along the edge that act as a strainer. Ducks forage for food underwater. When a duck raises its head, the food stays in its mouth while the water drains out. A Canada goose's bill is designed for grasping plants. Mergansers have narrow bills with notches perfect for holding the slippery fish they eat.

Migration

Of the world's 10,466 bird species, about 1,800 migrate. No one knows exactly what triggers migration each year. Ornithologists, scientists who study birds, believe it could be changes in day length, decreasing temperatures, and a decrease in food supplies. Another mystery is how the birds find their way to their summer and winter homes. Navigation by the sun, the stars, and Earth's magnetic field may play a role. Some people think birds also use their sense of smell to migrate.

Bird Migration Routes Between North and South America

Several birds you might see in your own backyard migrate south each winter. This map shows the routes some common birds take.

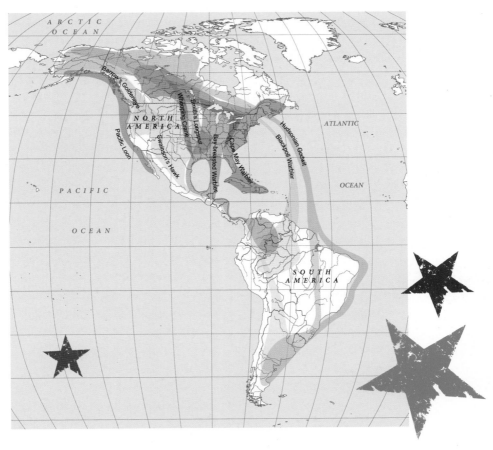

Birds and Oil Spills

Oil spills, such as the one in the Gulf of Mexico in 2010, are devastating to seabirds. It doesn't take a huge oil spill to harm seabirds and shorebirds. Even a small amount of oil, such as a spill from a boat's motor, can injure or kill a bird. If the oil reaches the beach, shorebirds that feed along the shoreline are also harmed.

Seabirds' feathers keep them warm and dry in the cold ocean. When oil spills into the water, the feathers are coated in a greasy slime. Then the feathers are no longer waterproof.

Because their feathers are no longer waterproof, birds coated in oil lose body heat and may die in the icy water. Coated birds try to get rid of the oil by preening their feathers. As they do this, they swallow some of the oil, which poisons and eventually kills them.

Workers can wash coated birds in soap and water and keep them safe until they are well enough to be released. But the problems are not over. Oil might wash up on important breeding areas, destroying critical habitats. Food sources can also be poisoned.

Whooping cranes spread
their wings wide during
a mating dance.

Courtship and Mating

Every spring, male and female birds come together to mate and raise young. Building a nest, protecting the eggs, and finding food for newly hatched chicks is a big job. In most bird species, a male and female stay together for the breeding season and share family responsibilities. Some birds find new mates each year. Others—such as Atlantic puffins, whooping cranes, and bald eagles—stay with the same mate throughout their lifetimes.

 Whooping cranes are the tallest North American birds.

Courtship

When spring comes, a male's first job is to attract a mate. The male peacock fans out his long and colorful tail train. Then he shakes his wing and tail feathers and calls out to a female. The male bowerbird builds an elaborate structure of sticks and twigs called a bower. He decorates it with stones, shells, flowers, dead beetles, and other prizes. If a female seems interested in his bower, he woos her with dances and songs.

A peacock's train can extend more than 3 feet (1 m) high.

A male weaver bird builds a nest and then hangs upside down from it, calling out in hopes of attracting a mate.

Nesting

Songbirds build simple cup-shaped nests, while African weaverbirds construct elaborate hanging nests. Nuthatches, hornbills, and some other birds use cavities in tree trunks for their homes. The female great hornbill seals herself and her eggs inside a cavity nest. She leaves a tiny slit so her mate can deliver food. The emperor penguin doesn't bother with a nest. The male holds a single egg on top of its feet, keeping it warm under folds of skin on its belly.

Raising Chicks

After hatching, most chicks are helpless. It takes both parents to protect and feed these hungry babies. Some birds, known as brood parasites, have found ways of making others do the work for them. The cuckoo finds a nest belonging to a different species where eggs have already been laid. The cuckoo removes an egg and lays one of her own in its place. The host mother returns and, not noticing the switch, incubates the egg with her own. When the chick emerges, she feeds and cares for it. She does not seem to realize that the cuckoo chick is much larger than her own chicks. In many cases, the strange chick is even larger than she is!

From Egg to Robin

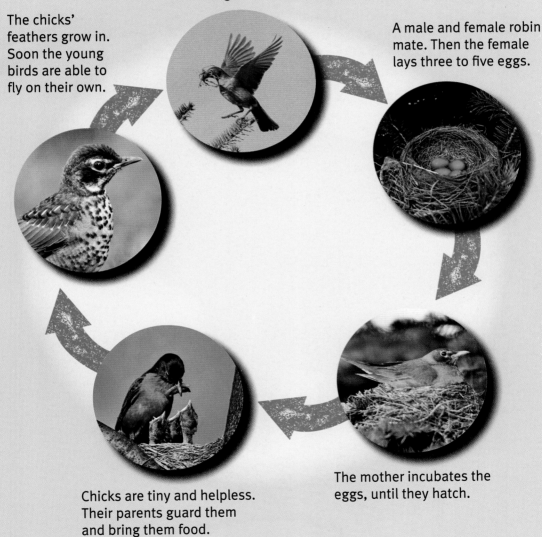

In the spring, the female robin begins to build a nest.

A male and female robin mate. Then the female lays three to five eggs.

The mother incubates the eggs, until they hatch.

Chicks are tiny and helpless. Their parents guard them and bring them food.

The chicks' feathers grow in. Soon the young birds are able to fly on their own.

Pigs and other nonnative species contributed to the extinction of the dodo, a flightless bird that lived on the island of Mauritius in the Indian Ocean.

Humans and Birds

All over the globe, bird populations are decreasing. In the past 500 years, more than 150 bird species and subspecies have become **extinct**. Some scientists think that hundreds more could disappear by the year 2100. In the past, the greatest threat was overhunting. Birds were killed for food or feathers. Another problem was the introduction of **invasive species**, such as rats and cats, where birds had previously encountered few predators.

 The last confirmed sighting of a living dodo bird was in 1662.

Parrots, such as these macaws, face not only vanishing habitats but also capture for the pet trade.

Vanishing Habitat

Worldwide, birds face habitat destruction. Tropical rain forests are home to many bird species. As forests are cleared for farms, pastures, and other developments, birds are left with smaller patches of habitat. Wetlands are drained to make way for other uses. This impacts herons, cranes, and other wetland birds. Sometimes birds, especially parrots, are taken from the wild and sold as pets. This is cruel to the captured birds and threatens wild bird populations.

Songbirds

Many people love observing birds in the wild. But bird-watchers don't just watch—they listen, too! Passerines are known for their songs. These are long, often complicated calls. Songs are used to attract mates or declare a bird's territory. Some species, such as the ovenbird, have only one song. Others have more. American robins sing around 70 songs. Mockingbirds (right) can learn to mimic, or copy, more than 200 other birds' songs. Brown thrashers might learn 2,000!

Our Warming Planet

Global warming affects birds as well. Some migrating species are shifting their ranges northward and beginning their spring migrations sooner. Robins arrive at nesting areas in the Rocky Mountains several weeks earlier than they did 20 years ago. Unfortunately, worms and other food are not available that soon in the spring, so these early birds have difficulty finding enough to eat.

Domestic cats kill an estimated 2.4 billion birds in the United States each year, including many robins.

Fruit-eating birds, such as cardinals, help disperse fruit seeds, which could grow into new plants.

Why Should We Care?

Birds and insects **pollinate** many plants. Birds also eat harmful insects and rodents that could otherwise destroy crops. They help protect forests by feeding on insect pests. Fruit-eating birds disperse seeds with their droppings, depositing seeds in areas where they might grow well. Humans use these fruits, forests, and crops for food and other products. The plants also help keep the earth healthy. We must protect birds not only for their sake but also for our own. ★

True Statistics

Average number of feathers on a songbird: 1,500 to 3,000

Number of feathers on a hummingbird, the least feathered bird: 940

Number of feathers on a swan, the most feathered bird: More than 25,000

Longest nonstop migration: 6,300 mi. (10,139 km), the bar-tailed godwit

Force needed to break an ostrich egg: 120 lb. (54 kg)

Weight of the bee hummingbird, the world's smallest bird: 0.056 oz. (1.6 grams)

Weight of the ostrich, the world's largest bird: Up to 330 lb. (149.7 kg)

Speed of the peregrine falcon, the fastest flying bird: 117 mph (188.3 kph) when diving

Wingspan of the wandering albatross: More than 11 ft. (3.4 m)

Did you find the truth?

F All birds migrate.

T All birds lay eggs.

Resources

Books

Alderfer, Jonathan K. *National Geographic Kids Bird Guide of North America: The Best Birding Book for Kids from National Geographic's Bird Experts*. Washington, DC: National Geographic, 2013.

Berger, Melvin, and Gilda Berger. *Birds*. New York: Scholastic, 2010.

Visit this Scholastic Web site for more information on birds:
★ www.factsfornow.scholastic.com
Enter the keyword **Birds**

Important Words

airfoil (AYR-foyl) — a surface shaped to provide enough lift when in motion to allow a body to fly

class (KLAS) — a group of related plants or animals that is larger than an order but smaller than a phylum

endothermic (en-duh-THURM-ik) — warm-blooded

extinct (ik-STINGKT) — no longer found alive

global warming (GLOH-bul WARM-ing) — a warming of Earth's atmosphere and oceans

incubated (ING-kyuh-bate-id) — kept eggs warm until they hatch

invasive species (inVAY-siv SPEE-sheez) — a plant or animal that is introduced to a new habitat and may cause that habitat harm

krill (KRIL) — small sea creatures that have an outer skeleton

plumage (PLOO-mij) — a bird's feathers, considered all together

pollinate (PA-luh-nate) — carry or transfer pollen from flowering plants to allow them to reproduce

preening (PREEN-ing) — using beaks to clean and arrange feathers

vertebrates (VUR-tuh-bruts) — animals that have backbones

Index

Page numbers in **bold** indicate illustrations

adaptations, 22, 23, 26, 27
Aves class, 15

babies. *See* chicks.
beaks, 8, 10, **22**, 23, 27
body temperatures, 16, 19, 25, 31
bones, **16**, 17
brood parasites, 36

chicks, **11**, 12, 21, 33, 36, **37**
colors, 7, **20**, 23, 34
communication, 23, 34, 41

eggs, **21**, 33, 35, 36, **37**
endothermic animals, 16
extinction, **38**, 39

feathers, **14**, 15, **19**, 20, 23, 25, **27**, **31**, **34**, 39
feet, 8, 12, 23, 27, 35
females, 20, 33, 34, 35, 36, 37
flippers, 8, 18, 23
flying, **9**, 13, **16**, **17**, **18**, 19, 21, 23
food. *See* insects; plants; prey.

habitats, **6**, 7, 9, 11, 15, 23, **24**, 25, 31, 40
hawks, 18, 22, 23
hummingbirds, **9**, **10**, 13, 15, 22
hunting, **8**, 18, 23, 39

incubation, 21, 35, 36, **37**
insects, **18**, 22, 23, 43

legs, 12, 16

males, 11, 12, **14**, 15, **20**, 33, **34**, **35**, 37
map, **29**

mating, **20**, 31, **32**, 33, 34, 37, 41
migration, **28**, **29**, 42

nests, **21**, 33, **35**, 36, **37**

oil glands, 25, **27**
oil spills, 30–**31**
ostriches, **11**–12, **13**, 15

passerines, 23, 25, **26**, 41
penguins, **6**, 7, **8**, 13, 15, 18, 23, 25, 35
people, 16, 31, 39, 40, 41, 43
perching birds. *See* passerines.
plants, **10**, 18, 22, 23, 27, 31, 33, **43**
populations, 39, 40
predators, 11–**12**, 39, 42
preening, **19**, 31
prey, 8, 23, 31, 33, **37**, **42**, 43
puffins, **17**, 33

robins, 23, **37**, 41, **42**

seeds, 22, 23, **43**
sizes, 13, 23, 26
skeletons. *See* bones.
songs, 23, 34, 41
species, 15, 20, 23, 26, 28, 33, 39, 40, 41
swimming, 7, **8**, 13, 23

tails, 8, **14**, 15, 19, **34**

vertebrates, 16

waterproofing, 25, **27**, 31
weight, 13, 17, 21, 22
wings, 8, **9**, 11, **16**, **18**, 19, 23, **32**, 34

About the Author

Ann O. Squire is a psychologist and an animal behaviorist. Before becoming a writer, she studied the behavior of rats, tropical fish in the Caribbean, and electric fish from central Africa. Her favorite part of being a writer is the chance to learn as much as she can about all sorts of topics. In addition to writing *Reptiles*, *Mammals*, and *Birds* in Scholastic's True Book series, Squire has written about many different animals, from lemmings to leopards and cicadas to cheetahs. She lives in Katonah, New York.

[10]